Public Planet Books

A Series Edited by Dilip Gaonkar
and Michael Warner

Public Planet Books is a series designed by writers in and outside the academy—writers working on what could be called narratives of public culture—to explore questions that urgently concern us all. It is an attempt to open the scholarly discourse on contemporary public culture, both local and international, and to illuminate that discourse with the kinds of narrative that will challenge sophisticated readers, make them think, and especially make them question. It is, most importantly, an experiment in strategies of discourse, combining reportage and critical reflection on unfolding issues and events—one, we hope, that will provide a running narrative of our societies at this particular *fin de siècle*.

Public Planet Books is part of the Public Works publication project of the Center for Transcultural Studies, which also includes the journal *Public Culture* and the Public Worlds book series.

Feminist Accused of Sexual Harassment

public planet books

Feminist Accused of Sexual Harassment

Jane Gallop

DUKE UNIVERSITY PRESS *Durham and London 1997*

Printed in the United States of
America on acid-free paper ∞
Typeset by Tseng Information
Systems, Inc. in Bodoni Book
Library of Congress Cataloging-
in-Publication Data appear on
the last printed page of this book.

For Dick, Max, and Chris

who loved me through the case

and criticized me through the writing.

And for Ruby,

hoping she will grow up to a world

where smart, powerful women are widely

held to be sexy.

Contents

1. Feminist Accused of Sexual Harassment

I am a feminist professor who was accused by two students of sexual harassment. This book is centered on that fact: the title is modeled after the style of tabloid headlines because of the way this fact lends itself to sensationalism. While any accusation of sexual harassment seems to promise a juicy scandal, this particular accusation is more sensational due to the newsworthy anomaly of a feminist being so accused. While sexual harassment is customarily a feminist issue, feminists usually appear on the accusers' side. For a feminist to be the accused is a dramatic reversal.

What kind of a feminist would be accused of sexual harassment?

I became a feminist early in 1971. It was, of course, the big moment for feminist awakenings, for young women around the country, around the world. At the time, we called it "women's liberation." Historians who remembered the women's movement of the nineteenth century called it "the second wave." And, although we baby boomers didn't think we were second to anyone or anything, it certainly was a wave, washing over my generation, soaking us through and through with a new understanding of who we were and what we could become, changing us forever.

I was halfway through college at the time. I did college in three years, in a special post-Sputnik program that recruited promising high-school kids from around the country and streamlined requirements to race us through; 1970–71 was the second of my three years, and I remember it all happening very fast, in a wonderful, dizzying jumble.

I was reading the books that everyone seemed to be reading, books not assigned for any course. I remember three in particular: Simone de Beauvoir's *Second Sex,* Kate Millett's *Sexual Politics,* and Shulamith Firestone's *Dialectic of Sex.* Serious, intellectual books, not unlike the books I was reading for courses. But because these were chosen, not assigned, read for reasons of social peer pressure and adolescent desire, they seemed very different.

The books were a big part of it, but I wasn't just reading, I was also going to meetings. Meetings of various sorts of women's groups, both on campus and downtown at the Women's Center. I don't remember the names of the groups or the purposes of the meetings, but I remember the feel of it all: the sense of being part of a community of women, the busy calendar, the sociability, the desire to belong, and my attraction to the strength and beauty of some of the women who went to the meetings.

The books and the meetings are inextricably jumbled together in my memory of that hectic period. There, on the fringes of my college education, I experienced an exhilarating mix of private reading and social community, which I would call learning, in the strongest sense of that word. Not only did it change me, but it vastly improved my life then and there in two essential and entwined ways.

Despite my academic "promise," which had gotten me into the fast-track foundation-funded experimental program, I was a poor student my first year of college. I got mediocre grades, did a minimum of work with little enthusiasm, cut classes, and either watched late late movies on TV or played bridge all night. My second year of school, I became a feminist, and I became a good student. Despite all the meetings, the social and political gatherings, I spent more time on my homework and attended classes more regularly. My senior year, I wrote an honor's thesis and really threw myself into that work, caring deeply about it. Somehow, feminism had made it possible for me to take my schoolwork seriously.

Freshman year, my disaffection as a student was

matched by my sexual passivity. As a good soldier in the sexual revolution, I had sex often, but with little pleasure and no orgasms. Although I fervently wished that all these young men I bedded would fall in love with me, all my wishing and hoping wasn't really desire.

Thanks to feminism, not only did I become a better student, but my sex life improved. In January 1971 I read de Beauvoir's *Second Sex,* learned that women could masturbate, and had my first orgasm. For me, that sea change will always be a central part of what "women's liberation" means. In no way did I lose interest in sex with other people, but now that meant bringing my sexuality into an encounter, rather than hoping some man could endow me with sexuality. I credit feminism with teaching me sexual pleasure.

Not only pleasure but also desire. A vocal if small lesbian presence was integral to the women's community on campus; this diffuse presence made the entire community seem a space of sexual possibility. I had the hots for so many of the energetic young women who went to the same meetings as I. While I actually slept with very few of them, these attractions introduced me to the feel of desire. Whereas my adolescent boy-craziness had filled me with romantic fantasies of love, when I thought about the women at the meetings I burned to touch their bodies. I walked around that year constantly in heat, energized for political activity and schoolwork; I learned that desire, even desire unacted upon, can make you feel very powerful. And the space where I learned desire—where it filled me with energy and drive—I call feminism.

I had been a "sexually active" young woman who was, ironically, neither sexual nor active but rather awash in romance and passivity. I had been a supposedly smart girl who was deeply alienated from her own desire for knowledge. Within one whirlwind year I came into a sense of my sexual power, of my sexuality as drive and energy. In that very same year I became an active, engaged student committed to knowing as much and as well as possible. I speak of these as if they were two transformations, but they are actually two aspects of the same transformation. One and the same change made me both an engaged, productive student and a sexually energized, sexually confident woman. The disaffected, romantic, passive young woman I had been gained access simultaneously to real learning and to an active sexuality. One achievement cannot be separated from the other.

This double transformation was my personal experience of what we then called "women's liberation." This access to learning and to pleasure will always be the root meaning, my most powerful personal sense of feminism. I know there are many people for whom feminism is the opposite of sexy. And even that there are many people who presume feminism to be anti-intellectual. But for me feminism will always name the force that freed me to desire and to learn.

My initial and formative experience of feminism was this entry into a milieu bubbling indiscriminately with ideas and lusts. *Feminism turned me on,* figuratively and literally: my body and my mind began firing, pulsing with energy, an energy that did not distinguish between mind and body. Feminism made me feel sexy and smart; feminism felt smart and very sexy. When I call myself a feminist, as I have for twenty-five years, I necessarily refer to that milieu where knowledge and sex bubble together, to that possible community, to that possibility for women.

Perhaps that is what makes me the kind of feminist who gets accused of sexual harassment.

Since being accused of harassment, I feel like my life has fallen into sensationalism. I've become a spectacle. Despite the urge to hide in shame, I've decided to speak from this sensational location. I'd like to make spectacle speak, to use spectacle to explore our assumptions about sexual harassment and feminism.

To do this, I have to tell what happened to me, tell how and why I was accused of harassment and what the investigation determined. But I won't be telling what happened chronologically; the story will appear broken into pieces and out of order. For spectacle to speak, it must be analyzed, broken down into its various components.

My purpose is not simply to tell my story but rather to use that story to understand what's going on with sexual harassment. The spectacle taught me a thing or two, and I'd like to try and explain what I've learned.

Feminist sexual harasser seems like a contradiction in terms. I find myself positioned at the center of this contradiction. Although the position has been personally quite uncomfortable, professionally I can see it as a rare vantage point, an opportunity to produce knowledge. I have long suspected that a contradiction in terms might present an occasion to confront and rethink the terms themselves.

As a feminist theorist of sexuality, I consider it my business to understand sexual harassment. And so I'd like to take advantage of my peculiar position as an accused harasser to provide a fresh feminist view of the issue. Theorizations of harassment generally focus on what is clearly the classic scenario: the male boss uses his professional clout to force himself upon a female subordinate—sleep with me or you'll lose your job, sleep with me and you'll get a raise, a promotion. Rather than refer to this classic case, I want to produce an understanding of sexual harassment based instead upon the limit case of a feminist so accused.

The classic scenario is explicit and quid pro quo (demand for sex in exchange for professional support). The concept of harassment also includes more implicit forms, where the sexual demand or the professional threat is not stated but understood. Implicit sexual demands might ultimately include any charged talk or behavior; implicit professional threats could possibly cover the entire range of professional interaction. While these possibilities are potentially already limitless, the range of harassment is also expanding in other directions. Harassment need not be perpetrated by bosses; peers can harass, even subordinates. And gender can be a variable: increasing numbers of cases involve a man claiming to have been harassed or a woman accused of harassment.

The classic scenario—easy to recognize and deplore as sexual harassment—expands its application in every direction. I want to ground my theorizing in a limit case precisely because I believe that there should be limits to this bloated general application. I hope that my example can expose the limitations of loose analogies and impede this rampant expansion of the concept of sexual harassment.

Feminism has a special relation to sexual harassment. One could in fact say that feminism invented sexual harassment. Not, of course, the behavior itself, which presumably has gone on as long as men have held power over women. But, until feminism named it, the behavior had no official existence. In the mid-seventies, feminism got women to compare notes on their difficulties in the workplace; it came out that women employees all too frequently had to cope with this sort of thing. Feminism named this behavior "sexual harassment" and proceeded to make it illegal.

Today the general public knows that sexual harassment consists of some form of unwanted sexual advances and that it is some sort of crime. Inevitably people assume that it is sex that makes harassment criminal. Feminism's interest in prosecuting harassment is then chalked up to feminism's supposed hostility to sex.

But, whatever the feelings of individual feminists, feminism is not in principle a movement against sexuality. It is, in principle and in fact, against the disadvantaging of women. Sexual harassment is a feminist issue not because it is sexual but because it disadvantages women. Because harassment makes it harder for women to earn a living, feminists declared it a form of discrimination against women. This framing was so persuasive that, within a few years, harassment was added to the legal definition of sex discrimination. Since discrimination on the basis of sex was already illegal, once harassment was included within the category of discrimination, it immediately became a crime. Sexual harassment is criminal not because it is sex but because it is discrimination.

When I was charged with sexual harassment, the accusations were made on official university forms that bore the heading "COMPLAINT OF DISCRIMINATION." Under that heading, the students filed formal complaints against me, checking the box marked "Sexual Harassment." This form includes twelve such boxes,

each pertaining to a type of discrimination (race or color, sex, national origin, etc.). The form itself makes it clear that harassment is treated as a subspecies of the general wrong, discrimination.

After reviewing the evidence and interviewing the witnesses, the university officer who investigated the charges against me was convinced that I had not in fact discriminated—not against women, not against men, not on the basis of sexual orientation, not on any basis whatsoever. She believed that my pedagogical practices had been, as she put it, applied in a consistent manner. Yet she nonetheless thought I probably was guilty of sexual harassment.

When it is possible to conceive of sexual harassment without discrimination, then sexual harassment becomes a crime of sexuality rather than of discrimination. There is, in fact, a recent national trend toward findings of sexual harassment where there is no discrimination. This represents a significant departure from the feminist formulation of harassment.

Although the shock value of my case resides in the supposition that it is impossible to be both a feminist and a harasser, the spectacle fascinates because it suggests the possibility that a feminist *could* be a sexual harasser—which would mean that either feminism or sexual harassment (maybe even both) are not what we assumed they were. A feminist sexual harasser is no longer a contradiction in terms; rather, it is the sign of an issue drifting from its feminist frame.

I was construed a sexual harasser because I sexualize the atmosphere in which I work. When sexual harassment is defined as the introduction of sex into professional relations, it becomes quite possible to be both a feminist and a sexual harasser.

The classic harassment scenario clearly involves both discrimination against women and sexualization of professional relations. Because people always refer to that classic case, it has been assumed that sexualizing the workplace is automatically disadvantageous to women. But if we base our thinking in the more exotic possibility of a feminist sexualizer, these two aspects of harassment no longer fit so neatly together. And sexualizing is not necessarily to women's disadvantage.

It is no coincidence that I happen to be both a feminist and someone whose professional relations are sexualized. It is because of the sort of feminist I am that I do not respect the line between the intellectual and the sexual. Central to my commitment as a feminist teacher is the wish to transmit the experience that brought me as a young woman out of romantic paralysis and into the power of desire and knowledge, to bring the women I teach to their own power, to ignite them as feminism ignited me when I was a student.

The chill winds of the current climate threaten to extinguish what feminism lit for me. What felt liberating to me as a student is today considered dangerous to my students. Today's antiharassment activism is, of course, a legacy of seventies feminism. But the antisexual direction of the current trend makes us forget how women's liberation turned us on. The present climate makes it easy to forget and thus crucial to remember. And so, at the risk of sounding as old as I am, I want to tell you again what feminism on campus felt like back when I was a student.

In 1971, there was a weekend-long feminist event on campus, lots of workshops and seminars, which combined teaching the issues and organizing us for activism. As part of this event, Saturday night there was a dance—women only, featuring a women's rock band (the first I'd ever seen).

Outraged at the idea of a women-only dance, male students came to crash the party. A large group of us women threw ourselves against the door. It was a thrill keeping the men out, feeling the power of our combined weight, heaping our bodies together in this symbolic enactment of feminist solidarity. And then, after the men gave up, we decided to celebrate our triumph, our women-only space by taking off our shirts and dancing bare-breasted.

Our breasts were political. In those days feminists were said to burn bras. Restricting and constraining movement, bras provided a metaphor for women's bonds. We didn't wear bras. We stripped off our shirts in triumphant defiance of the men we had kept out. With no men around to ogle our breasts, we were as free as men to take off our shirts in public; so we were asserting equal rights. But our breasts were not just political.

I remember Becca that night, a gorgeous young woman a year or so older than me. She had been one of the first to the door, expertly throwing her long, rangy body against the would-be intruders. And she was the first to take off her shirt and start dancing, revealing the most beautiful breasts I had ever seen. We all danced together in a heap, intoxicated with the joy and energy of our young feminism. The bacchanalian frenzy did not in the least cloud my focus on Becca's breasts. I was dancing with those beautiful breasts, dancing all the harder because I so wanted to touch those breasts.

While I'll never forget Becca's breasts, they were not the most memorable sight at the dance. Earlier that evening, two women had made a spectacular entrance. One of them taught my first women's studies course, which I was taking that semester. One of the campus's best-known feminists, an early leader in the national movement for women's studies, a published writer over six feet tall, this teacher was a woman whom I looked up to in every way. She walked into the dance accompanied by a beautiful girl I had seen around and knew to be a senior. The teacher was wearing a dress, the student a man's suit; their carefully staged entrance publicly declared their affair.

I thought the two of them were just the hottest thing I'd ever seen. I profoundly admired the professor; I found the senior girl beautiful and sophisticated. I wanted both of them. Although I would have loved to have an affair like theirs, I didn't feel left out and envious. I felt privileged to be let in on the secret. I felt it as our secret, the secret of our women's party.

This couple could no more safely appear around campus together like that than we could safely walk around with our shirts off. But the relationship could be revealed within our women-only space for the same reasons Becca could expose her breasts. Not because they weren't sexual, but because we as a community could recognize them as our sexuality, could affirm them as part of the new possibilities opened to us as women by feminism. The couple was performing *for us:* we were not only their special, exclusive audience, but they presented us with the spectacle of our daring communal possibility.

The long-haired senior was usually seen on campus in rather feminine clothes. Her getup that night was quite clearly meant for their joint appearance. Although their butch-femme attire functioned as a revelation, what it revealed was not some hidden sexual truth about them, but rather sexuality as the very possibility of taking on roles. In those days feminists saw social roles as traps, in particular masculine and feminine roles. We just recently liberated women were so afraid of being trapped by roles that we tended to embrace a broadly flattening egalitarianism. This couple walked in and implied that we didn't have to fear being obliterated by roles, that we were strong enough to take them on. And sexy enough to get off on them.

Although their costuming referred to male/female roles, their performance made us think of the roles they played outside that room: teacher and student. Perhaps, they seemed to be saying, teacher/student, like butch and femme, could be roles we explored for our pleasure and empowerment. It was crucial to this feminist spectacle that the student was the one wearing men's clothing. This seemed a role reversal. Her suit hinted that their connection made it possible for this student to take on power with the teacher. Our institutional roles did not have to limit our relationships, and they also did not have to be ignored in some colorless egalitarian utopia where all women were the same.

This was a performance custom-made for our community, using gender as a sexual metaphor to make explicit a possibility the community as a whole was exploring. Campus feminists came together in the context of feminism but also in the context of the university. In those days, feminism offered students the rare opportunity to mingle with faculty in a manner not circumscribed by our institutional roles.

Feminism was as new for our teachers as it was for us. We were all reading and being changed by the same books; we were going to the same political events and social gatherings. In the context of feminism, students and teachers worked and played together in some assumed commonality as women, a commonality that seemed to override the various social and institutional roles that separated us.

Not that our roles totally disappeared. What happened was more exciting and more empowering. We belonged to the same women's community as our teachers *and* we never stopped seeing them as teachers. It was heady indeed to attend meetings with faculty women, to feel part of a community with them. It made us feel like adults, like intellectuals, like we could in some way share in the aura of these knowledgeable, accomplished women. It was in this context, where faculty treated us as sister feminists rather than just as students, that I became a better student, a student who believed in my work, the sort of student who would ultimately become a professor.

This campus women's community was not just extracurricular. We didn't just happen to be teachers and students; we were actually interacting regularly in classroom situations. The feminist students were taking the new women's studies courses; the feminist faculty were teaching those courses. And for both students and faculty, these experimental new courses were the ones that really mattered.

We considered women's studies an academic wing of feminism where the learning that was liberating us could become part of the university curriculum. At the time, women's studies was not yet a formal program; a steering committee was set up to conceive its shape before we applied for official university status. The decision was made, on principle, to include students on what would more traditionally have been a faculty committee. As an undergraduate, I got to serve on the committee, and I felt privileged to be allowed to join the faculty in building women's studies. The inclusive composition of this committee betokened our vision of women's studies as different from the rest of the university: knowledge would be more egalitarian and more alive.

This commitment to a freer, less rigid knowledge

meant exploring new kinds of pedagogical relations. We didn't want teacher and student to be identities determining what we did and said; we hoped they could be roles we might take on for our benefit, roles that were sometimes useful, sometimes irrelevant. In our vision of a feminist university, we imagined teachers and students not separated by some uncrossable chasm, but joined in a shared pursuit of knowledge and women's liberation. And it was this brave if naive vision of faculty and students pursuing a new feminist relation to knowledge that I saw bodied forth in the spectacle of a feminist teacher-student affair.

I looked at this bold proclamation of sexuality and I saw my teacher, the one teaching my first women's studies course, which I was so excited about, which was changing my life for good. I saw one of the leaders of the movement for women's studies, not just on my campus but nationwide. And I didn't separate what I learned here about my teacher from the other ways I knew her. Her appearance at the dance became part of my image of my women's studies teacher and part of my image of women's studies.

That was the first time I ever thought of teacher-student sex in relation to feminism. And feminism shed a rosy glow over the prospect. Feminism provided the occasion to fantasize teacher-student sex alongside other brave new possibilities: from a women's rock band and dancing bare-breasted, to having the physical force to resist men's intrusion, to the dream of campus women of all ages and institutional ranks joining together to reshape the university and knowledge itself in the image of our feminist excitement.

Twenty-five years ago, I thought women's studies was hot. And since that time I've devoted myself to the feminist pursuit of knowledge. After college, I went on to graduate school and wrote a feminist dissertation. In the late seventies, I got a job teaching at a university, and I've been teaching women's studies courses ever since. In the eighties, I set up and ran a women's studies program at a college that did not yet have one. For more than two decades, I've been pursuing the dream of women's studies, led by my desire for the community that turned me on as a student.

Nowadays, women's studies is a lot older and more established; it doesn't feel so much like a bold experiment. While it still is said in women's studies circles that feminist teachers and students ought to have a nonhierarchical relation, ought to work together as sister seekers of knowledge, in fact the relation between feminist teachers and students is not what it was when women's studies was young. Students and faculty are no longer discovering feminism together; today, faculty who have been feminists for decades generally teach it to students for whom it is new. We are no longer discovering books together; instead, feminist faculty teach feminist classics we've read half a dozen times to students who are reading them for the first time. Whatever lip service we might still give to an egalitarian classroom, we function as feminist authorities, trying to get our students to understand a feminism we have long known. In this context, relations between us are defined much more by our roles as teacher and student than by any commonality as feminists. These days, rather than playing with our pedagogical roles, we seem to be trapped in them, our ability to connect as women very much limited by them.

Yet my students still want a feminist education that feels like women's studies did to me in 1971. And so do I, deeply. I want it for them and I want it still, again, for myself.

Sometimes it works. Sometimes a class or some more informal gathering suddenly comes together, and I feel the electricity, the buzz of live knowledge, the excitement of women thinking freely together. I always try to get us to that place where learning begins to dance. When we get there, my students love me and I'm crazy for them.

But when, as is more often the case, we don't get there, we are all disappointed. And then the students are likely to blame me.

For about a decade now, students in my feminist seminars have been complaining, in their anonymous evaluations, that I am "authoritarian." They expect a feminist teacher to be different, but my authority *as a feminist* feels too much like the male professor's authority in other classrooms. This experience of the feminist teacher as authority seems to betray the very principles of feminist teaching. In the context of feminism, these complaints of authoritarianism and the complaints of sexual harassment are saying the same thing: that I abuse my power, get off on my power at the students' expense, that I am just as bad as the men.

During the time I was under investigation by the university, the two graduate students who had filed the harassment complaints against me called a meeting of all the grad students in the department, a predominantly feminist group. The purpose of the meeting was to get the grad students to band together so they would be strong enough to curtail my power. At this student-only meeting, in the tradition of the feminist "speak-out," students shared with each other the abuses they had suffered at the hands of faculty.

And in that context, charges of sexual harassment mingled freely with complaints about other manifestations of power. Little distinction was made between sexual harassment (the criminal charge) and authoritarianism (a complaint about teaching style). In the eyes of the students gathered together to resist me and faculty oppression, they were virtually the same crime, the crime of having power over them.

Well-versed in antiharassment rhetoric, one of the

students states in her complaint against me: "it is at the level of the institutionally enforced power differential that I wish to locate my harassment charge." She found it humiliating that I had power over her and considered it a betrayal of feminism. Harassment for her in fact meant precisely experiencing what she calls "the power differential." Now that there are feminist faculty securely installed in the academy, students can experience feminist teachers as having power over them. And that makes it possible to imagine a feminist teacher as a sexual harasser.

Back when I was a student, our feminist teachers tended to be in rather tenuous institutional positions; they didn't have much institutional power. We didn't experience what power they did have as power over us, but rather as power for us—power for women, power for feminism. Bad power was men's power, the power society granted men to exploit women, impose upon women, abuse women. Twenty years later, thanks to feminism's academic success, students could look at me and see me as just like the men, just as bad as the men. And therefore worse.

A campus activist against sexual harassment, a student from another department who had never even met me, was quite willing to comment on my case to a reporter: "Jane Gallop is as bad as—*no, worse than*—the men who do this kind of thing." A woman "as bad as the men" is inevitably, *because she is a woman,* considered to be worse than the men. Although several men in my department have been accused of sexual harassment, none of those cases prompted students to rally against the accused.

Feminists often condemn the woman who is like a man as a traitor to feminism, a traitor to her sex. But the condemnation of what feminists call "the male-identified woman" bears an uncanny resemblance to a larger social prejudice, the vilification of women who are like men. Feminism has taught us a lot about that sexist image, how it works to limit and constrain women, to keep us in line, but feminists are not themselves always immune to it.

And what it means for a woman to be "just like a man" always comes down to two things: sex and power.

In 1993, at the very moment I am under investigation, Michael Crichton writes *Disclosure,* the first popular novel about sexual harassment. This novel by a best-selling author, a book that became almost immediately a Hollywood movie, marks a turning point: harassment has taken root in the culture's imagination. Sexual harassment moves from the news to the novel. And mainstream culture's first attempt to imagine harassment conjures up, not the classic scenario, but a male victim and a female predator.

Disclosure sports the epigraph, "Power is neither male nor female," and this view of power seems to be behind the choice to portray a role-reversal harassment. The epigraph is actually spoken within the novel. The woman lawyer who functions as the book's authority on harassment explains to the male victim: "the figures suggest that women executives harass men in the same proportion as men harass women. Because the fact is, harassment is a power issue. And power is neither male nor female. Whoever is behind the desk has the opportunity to abuse power. And women will take advantage as often as men." This sounds like the moral of a story about a female sexual harasser.

Crichton is a writer known for the extensive research behind his books, and this one is no exception: *Disclosure*'s understanding of harassment is very up-to-date. Explanations of sexual harassment are beginning to move away from the idea that gender is the key factor and toward a gender-neutral notion of power. While a number of feminists have embraced this move, I consider it to be a serious departure from feminism.

Sexual harassment was originally understood within a more general feminist analysis of sexism. Feminists saw that the specific power men exercise over individual women—as a boss or a teacher, say—is enormously magnified by widespread societal assumptions that men should dominate women. In a society that expects male sexuality to be aggressive and female sexuality submissive, a boss can sexually harass his female employee with a devastating combination of economic, psychological, and social coercion. The boss's pressure on his employee is backed not only by literal economic power and general psychological intimidation, but also by social expectations that relations between the sexes are supposed to be like this.

When we move beyond the gender configuration of the classic harassment scenario, some important things change. The link between sex and power is not always the same. Whereas male heterosexuality in our culture connotes power, both homosexuality and female sexuality tend to signify weakness and vulnerability. If we imagine a sexual harassment scenario where the victim is male or the culprit female, the abuse of power would not be reinforced by society's sexual expectations. Outside novelistic turnabouts (and Hollywood fantasies featuring Demi Moore), a woman is much more likely to undermine than to enhance her authority by bringing her sexuality into the professional domain.

Not unlike *Disclosure*, my accuser locates harassment "at the level of the institutionally enforced power differential." Both reflect a current trend in thinking about harassment that reduces power to mere institutional position. And thus forgets the feminist insight that the most destructive abuses of power occur because of widespread, deeply rooted social and psychological reinforcement.

Troubled by this move to a gender-neutral understanding of sexual harassment, I take *Disclosure* as a dramatic portrayal of its real danger. Rather than worrying about male exploitation and women's disadvantage, the novel's reader is confronted with the image of an evil woman; the reader identifies with and fears for the poor man she preys upon. Under the guise of despising sexual harassment, we find ourselves once again vilifying women who presume to be sexual and powerful like men are.

Embracing a gender-neutral formulation of harassment, we leave behind the concern with sexism only to find ourselves faced with something quite traditionally sexist: an image of a woman who is evil precisely because she is both sexual and powerful. Meredith Johnson, *Disclosure*'s villainess, is a single career woman who is sexy and sexually aggressive, professionally adept and successful. She corresponds to the pop-cultural image of a liberated woman. Although feminists have condemned women who are just like men, society at large tends to think of women who are like men as "feminists." We might see Meredith Johnson as the fantasy of a feminist sexual harasser.

Disclosure marks a real turning point in the response to sexual harassment. Or maybe a turn of the screw. As outrage at sexual harassment becomes popular, a role-reversal fantasy allows a wide audience to embrace the feminist issue of sexual harassment and at the same time turn it against liberated women.

As the century draws to a close, it appears that the campaign against sexual harassment may, in fact, be *the* success story of twentieth-century feminism. At a moment when abortion rights are endangered, when affirmative action is becoming unfashionable, when everyone is jumping on the family values bandwagon, when few women want to be thought of as feminists, there is a broad-based consensus that sexual harassment is despicable, and measures against it have become very popular.

Although feminists targeted sexual harassment in the 1970s, outrage against it did not become popular until the nineties. The Hill-Thomas hearings in late 1991 are generally credited with producing this effect. Although I have my own suspicions about the way that a black man makes it easier for the majority to see male heterosexuality as a threat to the social order, my concern here is rather with the more general question of how sexual harassment is understood at the moment when the nation finally rallies against it.

While the battle against sexual harassment has been feminism's great victory, I'm afraid that's because it has been too easy to separate the issue from feminism. Feminists took up the issue because we saw it as a form of sex discrimination, but sexual harassment is increasingly understood as having no necessary link to either discrimination or gender.

In 1990, Billie Wright Dziech, a national authority on sexual harassment, predicted that "genuine change can occur only when sexual harassment is approached as a professional rather than a gender issue." Three years later, the change Dziech was calling for seems to have occurred. Crichton's *Disclosure* approaches harassment in just that way: gender doesn't matter, what matters is who is "behind the desk." That same year, a university official finds it possible that I could be guilty of sexual harassment without having discriminated against anyone. The university's lawyer comments that they must take care to punish me as harshly as the men so that the university won't be accused of sex discrimination.

By the end of 1993, Dziech announces that the discussion of sexual harassment has entered a "new phase": the issue has moved beyond its feminist framework and taken on a life of its own. Although feminism brought the problem to public awareness, the larger public does not necessarily share the feminist assessment of the problem. Once separated from the issue of sex discrimination, harassment can be linked to other versions of socially undesirable sexuality.

As sexual harassment breaks loose from its feminist formulation, the crusade against it might even become not just independent of feminism, but actually hostile to feminism. Dziech envisions one particularly chilling possibility: "eventually the political right will embrace protections against sexual harassment as part of its agenda for a return to traditional values." A return to traditional values always implies women returning to our proper place. And then we might see not just the odd spectacle of a feminist accused of sexual harassment but the more general prospect of feminists being so accused precisely *because* we are feminists. Once sexual harassment is detached from its feminist meaning, it becomes possible to imagine feminism itself accused as a form of sexual harassment.

2. Consensual Amorous Relations

Just last week, I was gossiping with a friend of mine about the department she teaches in. My friend, who is a feminist, confessed that she supported a junior colleague "even though he is a sexual harasser." Being pretty sensitive about the issue, I confronted her: "Is he really a sexual harasser, or does he just date students?"

She only meant that he dated students. Thanks to an administrative stint, my friend is very familiar with academic policy. Her casual use of the term "sexual harasser" was not aberrant but, in fact, represents a new sense of sexual harassment operative in the academy today.

Nowadays, most campus sexual-harassment policies include a section on "consensual relations" between teachers and students. These range from outright prohibitions of teacher-student relationships to warnings that a consensual relationship will not protect the teacher from the student's claims of harassment.

Although the range suggests some uncertainty about the status of consensual relations, *their very inclusion within harassment policies* indicates that consensual relations are themselves considered a type of sexual harassment.

Sexual harassment has always been defined as *unwanted* sexual attention. But with this expansion into the realm of consensual relations, the concept can now encompass sexual attention that is reciprocated and very much welcome. This reconfigures the notion of harassment, suggesting that what is undesirable finally is not unwelcome attention but sexuality per se. Rather than some sexuality being harassing because of its unwanted nature, the inference is that sexuality is in and of itself harassment.

I have reason to be sensitive to this slippage in meaning. When I was accused of sexual harassment by two students, my relation to one of the complainants was deemed to be in violation of the university's policy on "consensual relations."

The two students charged me with classic quid pro quo sexual harassment. They both claimed that I had tried to get them to have sex with me and that, when they rejected me, I had retaliated by withdrawing professional support (in one case with negative evaluations of work, in the other with a refusal to write letters of recommendation). The university's affirmative-action office conducted a lengthy investigation which resulted in a pretty accurate picture of my relations with these students. I had not tried to sleep with them, and all my professional decisions regarding them seemed clearly based in recognizable and consistent professional standards. No evidence of either "sexual advances" or "retaliations" was to be found.

What the investigation did find was that I indulged in so-called sexual behavior that was generally matched by similar behavior directed toward me on the part of the students. Not only did they participate in sexual banter with me, but they were just as likely to initiate it as I was. With one of the students, this banter was itself so minimal that the case was dismissed. But because my relationship with the other complainant was much more elaborate, it was determined that this mutual relationship of flirtatious banter and frank sexual discussion violated the consensual-relations policy.

The woman who conducted the investigation thought that because I had a consensual "sexual relation" with a student, I should be considered guilty of sexual harassment. My lawyer argued that if this were a consensual relation, I was at most guilty of violating a university policy, not of breaking the federal law prohibiting harassment. While campus harassment policies increasingly encompass consensual relations, the laws that make harassment illegal not only do not concern themselves with such mutual relations, but would seem specifically to exclude them.

This confrontation between my lawyer and the university investigator (both specialists in the area of discrimination) demonstrates the gap opening up between a general understanding of harassment as unwanted sexual attention and this new sense of harassment operating in the academy today—which includes all teacher-student sexual relations, regardless of the student's desires.

After the investigation had been conducted, but before the findings were released, the university hired a lawyer from off-campus to head the affirmative-action office. It was she who wrote the final determination of my case. This lawyer found no probable cause to believe that I had sexually harassed anyone. But her determination does go on to find me guilty of violating university policy because I engaged with one of my students in a "consensual amorous relation."

The document explains the choice of "amorous" (a word that appears in the policy) as denoting a relation that was *"sexual" but did not involve sex acts.* Much less serious than quid pro quo harassment (trading professional support for sexual favors), less serious than hostile-environment harassment (discrimination by emphasis on sexuality), less serious even than consensual *sexual* relations, the precise finding of "consensual amorous relations" is, in fact, the slightest infraction comprised within the policy.

It was as if I had been accused of "first-degree harassment," and the charge had been reduced to something like "fourth-degree harassment." The distinction between sexual harassment and consensual relations becomes not a difference in kind but merely a difference in degree. The university found no evidence of compromised professional judgments, or of discrimination, unwanted sexual attention, or any sort of harassment; it found I wasn't even having sex with students. But the investigation revealed that I did not in fact respect the boundary between the sexual and the intellectual, between the professional and the personal. It was as if the university, seeing what kind of relations I did have with students, felt I must be *in some way* guilty and was able, through this wrinkle in the policy, to find me *slightly guilty of sexual harassment.*

The presumption on campuses today is that any sexual relation between a teacher and a student constitutes sexual harassment. One of our most esteemed universities explains: "What might appear to be consensual, even to the parties involved, may in fact not be so." The contrast here between "appearance" and "fact" suggests that so-called consensual-relations policies are *not in reality* about consensual relations, but about relations that are only *apparently* consensual. The policies assume that there is, in fact, no such thing as a consensual relation between a teacher and a student.

The policy of another major university elaborates:

"The respect and trust accorded a professor by a student, as well as the power exercised by the professor in giving praise or blame, grades, recommendations, etc., greatly diminish the student's actual freedom of choice. Therefore, faculty are warned against even an apparently consenting relationship. The administration involved with a charge of sexual harassment shall be expected to be unsympathetic to a defense based upon consent when the facts establish that a professional power differential existed within the relationship."

Students do not have full freedom of choice; thus their consent is not true consent but merely the appearance of consent. The very existence of "a professional power differential" between the parties means a relationship will not be treated as consensual, regardless of whether consent was in fact granted. Because students cannot fully, freely, and truly consent, all teacher-student relations are presumed to be instances of sexual harassment.

As a teacher of feminist theory, I recognize this critique of consent. It is based on a radical feminist critique of heterosexuality. Students cannot "really" consent to sex with professors for the same reasons that women cannot "really" consent to sex with men. Feminists saw that economic arrangements make heterosexuality generally "compulsory" for women. In a society where women are economically disadvantaged, most women must depend upon sexual relations with men (ranging from legal marriage to literal prostitution) for economic survival. If women need to have sex with men in order to survive, their consent to these sexual relations is not freely given.

There has been a good deal of confusion about what this critique of compulsory heterosexuality means. A few feminists have taken it to mean that no women *really want* to have sex with men. This then slides into the injunction that any woman who wants to be free *should not* have sex with men. Although only a very small number of feminists have ever taken this position, a lot of people have mistaken this extreme opinion for *the* feminist line. This confusion has resulted in widespread outrage at the idea that feminism would deny women the right to desire and enjoy men.

The feminist critique of compulsory heterosexuality was not meant to be a condemnation of heterosexuality per se but only of the way society forces men upon women without regard for our desire. Most feminists, in fact, understand this critique as an attempt to distinguish between socially coerced heterosexuality and women's actual desires for men. The crucial question is whether women are treated as mere sex objects or whether we are recognized as desiring subjects.

University administrators who piously intone against teacher-student sex, citing the student's impossibility to freely grant consent, would be shocked if they knew their position was based in a critique of the institution of marriage. And I don't think you could get them to agree to policies likewise prohibiting heterosexuality on the grounds that the power differential means a woman's consent is always to some extent coerced. Yet campuses around the country are formulating and enforcing policies that are the equivalent of the much-decried and seldom-embraced fringe feminist injunction against women sleeping with men.

As a feminist, I am well aware of the ways women are often compelled to sexual relations with men by forces that have nothing to do with our desire. And I see that students might be in a similar position with relation to teachers. But, as a feminist, I do not think the solution is to deny women or students the right to consent. Denying women the right to consent reinforces our status as objects rather than desiring subjects. That is why I believe the question of whether sexual advances are *wanted* is absolutely crucial.

Prohibition of consensual teacher-student relations is based on the assumption that when a student says yes she really means no. I cannot help but think that this proceeds from the same logic according to which when a woman says no she really means yes. The first assumption is protectionist; the second is the very logic of harassment. What harassment and protectionism have in common is precisely a refusal to credit women's desires. Common to both is the assumption that women do not know what we want, that someone else, in a position of greater knowledge and power, knows better.

I think back to that jubilant feminist dance I attended in 1971. Although sexual harassment was not a phrase we used in those days, unwanted sexual attention would pretty well describe the behavior of the guys who came to crash the party. They had, in fact, come with the explicit purpose of harassing us. Yet today, the notion of sexual harassment more likely would be applied to the mutually desirable relation between my women's studies teacher and the student who was her date to the dance.

When I think of that dance, I balk at the idea that teacher-student sex is synonymous with harassment. I remember the feminist student I was, what I wanted and what I didn't want, and I remember that it was precisely my sense of knowing what I did and didn't want that made me feel strong.

A year or so after that dance I began graduate school. My first semester there, feminist graduate students and faculty in the department recognized that I was a feminist and invited me to join a consciousness-raising group they were forming. It was in many ways a typical consciousness-raising group: in comparing our experiences we began to see them as not merely individual but as the shared experience of women. But in our case, there was even greater similarity because we were all women in the same department.

A student in the group was dating a professor while two of us were taking his graduate seminar. When we discussed our sex lives, I listened to what she said with more than the usual curiosity. No one in that feminist group thought their relationship inappropriate and, although it was titillating to have this access to private information about him, I don't believe it substantially added to or undermined his professional authority.

The group functioned not only politically, intellectually, and personally; it also became the core of our social life. I became close friends with two of the women in the group, women who remained my closest friends all through graduate school—one was a graduate student, the other a young professor. Around the group proper, a larger social circle formed, as we socialized not only with each other but with each other's friends and lovers.

This larger social circle brought together graduate students and junior faculty, women and men of both statuses. Our clique included two of the teachers who most mattered to me at the time. Both men in their thirties, not long out of graduate school themselves, these two turned me on to the latest ideas in the field I was studying—this was the cutting edge. These guys were brilliant: I wanted to do work that would impress them, and I wanted more than anything to be like them.

I was fortunate to have both of them on my dissertation committee. I pursued and developed personal relations with each of them. At the time, one was single, the other divorced; both were socially available. I met each of them frequently for lunches and dinners, coffees and drinks. I helped one move into a new apartment; I spent the day at the other's house watching a tennis tournament on TV. I wanted ever so badly to sleep with these guys. And I did my utmost to seduce them.

Both of them turned me down, more than once. But over the years, I did what I could to sway them. Trying not to be too obnoxious, I watched for opportunities that might present themselves, prepared to take advantage and press my suit. During my last year of graduate school, the year I was writing my thesis, I finally managed to have sex with them (each separately, to be sure, but oddly, coincidentally, in the same week).

I had sex but once with each of them. Neither of these became "relationships." It was just what is called "casual sex," although there was nothing casual about my relation to either of them. Their opinion of me already mattered profoundly; their teaching had forever changed the way I understood the world.

To be honest, I think I wanted to get them into bed in order to make them more human, more vulnerable. These two had enormous power over me: I don't mean their institutional position but their intellectual force. I was bowled over by their brilliance; they seemed so superior. I wanted to see them naked, to see them as like other men. Not so as to stop taking them seriously as intellects (I never did), but so as to feel my own power in relation to them.

Screwing these guys definitely did not keep me from taking myself seriously as a student. In fact, it seemed to make it somewhat easier for me to write. Seducing them made me feel kind of cocky and that allowed me to presume I had something to say worth saying.

It never occurred to me to worry that sex would prevent them from responding professionally to my work. Both men continued to serve on my dissertation committee. And they continued to serve me well, to offer vital criticism as well as encouraging praise, helping to make the thesis as good as possible, devoting considerable time and effort to responding to my writing. In other words, these men did not treat my work any differently than before we had sex.

Sexual harassment creates an environment that is hostile to a student's education. My experience was the opposite. I was in an environment extremely conducive to my education, a heady atmosphere where close personal contact intensified my desire to learn and my desire to excel. I learned and excelled; I desired and I fucked my teachers.

And they taught and challenged me, criticized and praised me; they let me see them as men and never stopped taking me seriously as a student. I felt that in their eyes I was both a desirable woman and a serious scholar. And thus I believed I could be both; I didn't feel I had to choose one at the expense of the other.

Fifteen years later, when I became aware that campuses were "protecting" students by banning student-teacher relations, I felt my desire erased and the way it had made me feel powerful denied. Although I am aware that not all such liaisons are so empowering for the student, I also know that my experience was far from unique. Lots of other smart, ambitious young women, many of them likewise feminist academics today, have felt powerful because they seduced their teachers.

Experience like mine is currently invisible. In the general consensus that student-teacher relations demean and debase the student, an entire stretch of women's experience is being denied, consigned to silence. And it just happens to be women's experience of feeling powerful and sexy, smart and successful.

After graduate school, I got a job at a medium-sized state university in a small college town. In the late seventies, the academic job market was tight: one took whatever job one could get (such is very much the case again today). I moved to this dinky little town where there wasn't really anything else but the university. It seemed like everyone in town was either under twenty-two or married; it didn't look like there would be much in the way of romantic possibilities.

My first year there, I taught a summer course; a graduate student from another department enrolled. He happened to live in the same apartment complex as I did, and sometimes I ran into him out by the pool. He was two years older than me and going through a divorce. A couple weeks into the term, he asked me if I wanted to go out on Friday night. Living in that town, I hadn't had a date in quite a while, so I was happy to accept his invitation.

We dated for the rest of the summer term. I don't think it affected my judgment of his work or my treatment of the other students in class. But I will admit both of us found our secret titillating: it was a perverse thrill to treat him in class just like the other students though all the while we also had this sexual relation outside of class.

We continued dating through the fall. I enjoyed spending time with him, but he wanted a more serious relationship and began pressuring me to live with him. By January, I gave in and let him move into my apartment. In April, I went out of town for the weekend to present a paper at an academic conference. While I was gone, he started sleeping with another woman. Although I was not in love with him, I was very attached to his companionship and desperate to hang on to him. I couldn't do it: by the time classes ended in May, he had moved out of my apartment and in with her.

I felt rejected and quite alone. One day, shortly after he moved out, I ran into an undergrad who had been in my class during the spring semester. This cute kid was intense and eccentric and one of the students most keyed into my teaching. He was excited to run into me off-campus; I was pretty down; it did me good to feel admired. During the semester, I had invited his class to my place for a party; so he had met the grad student who lived with me and now asked after him. I blurted out that he had just dumped me for another woman. That evening the undergrad stopped by my apartment. His idea was to cheer me up by sleeping with me. I was glad he had come by and immediately took to the idea.

We had sex on several other occasions over the course of the next year or so. This was, however, not at all a romantic relationship; all the sex was very casual. For example, about a year later he stopped by in just the same way he had the first time: it was my birthday, and, in view of the occasion, he wanted to make sure I got laid. The thought was sweet; I appreciated and accepted his offer.

But his real devotion to me was intellectual. He took every course he could with me during the rest of his time in college, began to read my scholarly articles, and generally tried to learn what I was trying to teach.

He even went so far as to take a women's studies course from me, although he had never shown any interest in feminism. This was my first women's studies course and, although I was touched dear Scott signed up, he was not the audience it was actually aimed at.

As expected, most of the students in that class were women, many of whom were feminists, a rarity among the conservative students at that school. A lesbian couple enrolled, the first out lesbians I had run into in my three years there. The two of them were delightful: it wasn't just that they both were smart, hip, and really good-looking, but they enjoyed performing their relationship in public, flaunting their sexuality to the discomfiture of the very straight student body.

The couple adopted me as their pet teacher, and as I thoroughly admired them, I was tickled to be so chosen. On weekends they would take me with them to the nearest lesbian bar, an hour's drive from the college town. Or they would come by in the evening with a bottle of wine, and the three of us would talk till the wee hours, as the atmosphere thickened with unspoken fantasies of transgressive possibility. One night they giddily confided that every time they passed my apartment building they would jokingly suggest "SBFJ." After making me beg repeatedly for explication, one of them finally whispered that the joke's abbreviation stood for "Stop By, Fuck Jane."

In the middle of that semester, they broke up. Late

one weekday evening soon after, the tough, curly-haired one showed up at my apartment with the express purpose of seducing me. I didn't know they'd broken up and was surprised both by her visit and by her intentions. But, since I found her very sexy, I was thrilled to let her seduce me. We spent the night enacting the unspoken fantasies of months of heady conversations. She was even sexier than I'd imagined.

It was morning when she left my place. That afternoon I was giving a public lecture on campus, previewing the book I was then writing, a book whose publication would soon make my career as a feminist theorist (a book called, incidentally, *The Daughter's Seduction*). The lecture was a triumph: the large room was full; the assembled colleagues and students were quite enthusiastic about my new work.

Sitting right up in the front row was Micki, my brash young seducer. Not herself a very serious student, caring rather more about her career as a singer/guitarist, Micki was not, in fact, particularly interested in my work. But she was turned on by the crowd's response to my presentation. Bursting with the sense of having possessed me but a few hours earlier, she looked like the proverbial cat who'd eaten the canary.

Her aim had been conquest: she had gotten what she wanted and given me a lot of pleasure in the process. It was a classic one-night stand, intensely tied to the moment. Although that was the extent of our sexual connection, we remained friendly. A month or so later, she invited me to come hear her perform at a local coffeehouse; it was my turn to be in her audience, my turn to be proud to know her.

Whatever role Micki's dalliance with me might have played in her breakup with Diane, it didn't seem to have any negative effect on Diane's relation to me. A year later, Diane found occasion to invite me to spend the night with her. Diane was soulful and very beautiful; I was extremely flattered and more than happy to accept her invitation.

With Diane too, sex was a one-night affair, but I remained her teacher well past that encounter. In contrast with Micki, Diane *was* a serious student. During her last semester of college, two years after her first class with me, she enrolled in the senior seminar I taught for graduating women's studies students. She did excellent work in that seminar, we worked together productively, and our relation both in and out of class seemed, as far as I could tell, unaffected by our erotic history.

By the time I taught that senior seminar in the spring of 1982, I no longer was having affairs with students. And I haven't slept with a student since then. Not, however, because of any change in my views about teacher-student liaisons. The reason lies rather in a change in my personal situation: by 1982 I was madly in love with the man I'm still happily with today. Over the years we've been together, he's taught me ever so much and been more than willing to learn from me; but he was never, strictly speaking, either my teacher or my student.

The stories I have just told portray human relations. In these affairs, my motivations as well as the motivations of the students are profoundly—sometimes sadly, sometimes sweetly—human. They span the usual range of reasons why people make contact: loneliness, sympathy, rebounding from a recently failed relationship, and, of course, admiration. I hope this gallery can give a sense of the diversity and humanity of such relations.

The stories also run the gamut of teaching relations: from intense, serious connections where the student's way of thinking is centrally transformed by the teaching, to very casual encounters where the teaching is pretty much marginal to the student's concerns. In my experience, the teaching relation remained essentially the same after sex: the casual students continued not to care particularly about the teaching; the serious students continued to take the teaching seriously and to be taken seriously as students by the teacher.

As I gather these experiences together—and place them in proximity to my seduction of my own teachers—I notice one consistency. In every instance, it was the student who made the first move; it was always the student who initiated sexual activity. This certainly runs counter to the cliché of the lecherous professor putting the moves on innocent young things. To be sure, I'm not trying to claim that teachers never make the first move; but that is not my experience. And I've had my share of experience, both as student and as teacher.

Although I no longer actually have sex with students, I still embrace such relations in principle. I resist the idea that what I did was wrong, and persist in seeing these liaisons as part of the wide range of sexual opportunities that I sampled as fully as possible in my younger days.

As someone who came of age during the sexual revolution, my teens and twenties were full of short-term serious romances and an even larger number of casual sexual encounters. This variety of experience was particularly good for me as a young intellectual woman, making me feel bold and forceful as well as desirable, helping me view the world as a place of diverse possibility. Especially for women pursuing the life of the mind, desire is a blessing rather than an insult. My desire gave me drive and energy; being an object of desire made me feel admired and wanted, worthy and lovable. Now long past my twenties, I am still convinced that desire is good and that when mutual desire makes itself felt, it is a very fine thing indeed.

Prohibitions against teacher-student relations seem based in a sense of sex as inherently bad. Sex for me is not some wholly separate, nasty, debased thing, but belongs more to the world of conversation and friendship, where people make contact with others who seem interesting, forceful, attractive. Because I value human connection above all else, I regard sex as a considerable good.

I think of my students primarily as people. As with people in general, I don't like some of them, I'm indifferent to many, and I find some of them especially admirable, congenial, or engaging. Although an awareness of our institutional roles definitely gave my affairs with students a certain pleasurable edge of transgression, I slept with students for essentially the same reasons I slept with other people—because they engaged me as human beings, because a spark of possibility lit between us.

It is ironic that relations between teachers and students have been banned as part of the fight against sexual harassment. We fight against sexual harassment precisely because it's dehumanizing, but the ban on consensual relations is dehumanizing too. Telling teachers and students that we must not engage each other sexually ultimately tells us that we must limit ourselves to the confines of some restricted professional transaction, that we *should not treat each other as human beings.*

Around 1990 I began to take loud and public exception to the new consensual-relations policies. I felt free to do so precisely because I hadn't been having sex with students since long before these policies came into existence. I thought I could risk opposing these policies because I was not in fact violating them.

This was, of course, before I found myself charged with sexual harassment. Two years after I started protesting these policies, the complaints against me were filed. A year after that, the university officially declared that I had violated its consensual-relations policy. Thus, I was found in violation of the very policy I had set about to protest.

I thought I was protesting a policy banning the sort of relations I used to have. I had not realized it was possible to apply the policy to the sorts of relations I still have with students.

Back in the days when I was sleeping with students, all the sex had taken place within a larger context of social and personal relations. For example, in that summer-school class where I started dating the grad student, there was another student, a female undergrad, that I used to hang out with. She had great style, and I loved to go shopping for clothes with her. Or we'd go drinking and compare notes on the difficulties of dating men. The next year, while I rarely had sex with Scott, I often went uptown to a bar with him and his friends to play pinball. And my relation to Micki and Diane began as a friendship with a couple; at the time none of us expected the couple to break up. The drinking and talking, or going out on a weekend, was not unlike relations I had with other students.

I have such relations with students to this day, although now mainly with graduate students. I socialize with students in groups and singly: we might go out to dinner, play tennis, or see a movie. Or one of my graduate advisees will tell me about his love life while I thoroughly enjoy giving him advice. Some of my best friends are students. Even though I no longer have sex with students, my relations with students have not really changed at all.

Some of these personal relations remain pretty casual; but others get intense, complicated, and sticky. The intense relations involve students who take me very seriously as a teacher. These are students who want, in some way, to be intellectuals or academics like I am. And these are the students I most care about as a teacher.

It was indeed just such a relation that landed me in violation of the school's consensual-relations policy. When this graduate student took her first course from me, immediately after the second class meeting she came up and asked if we could talk. I told her to come to my office hours the next morning, but she didn't want to wait and pressed me to meet with her right then. Seeing how important it was to her, I relented and went with her to my office, despite the fact that it was

9:30 P.M. When we got there, she didn't even sit down but blurted out that she wanted me to be her advisor. She was jittery with excitement, and I was tickled to see someone who wanted that much to work with me. I immediately agreed to be her advisor; she was overjoyed and asked if we could go to the bar across the street to talk. Flattered by the ardor of her desire to work with me, I again agreed. And so began a relationship that involved not only working together in class and in my office, but going out for drinks and dinners, sometimes with other students or with her girlfriends, sometimes just the two of us.

Right from the start the relationship was not just professional, not even just social, but intensely personal and personally intense. She was, by her own admission, enamored of my work before she even met me. An ambitious woman with a flair for outrageous performance, she identified with me and thought I'd be the ideal teacher for her. I responded strongly to her desire for a career like mine. The relationship was charged with energy. And was, as such crucial relations often are, difficult. Because I believe that the most powerful educational experiences occur in an atmosphere of such intensity, I welcomed it, even though I often found it personally challenging.

I have had other teaching relationships that were as or more personal and intense. Although always tricky, they generally produce excellent results: I see the students consistently learn a lot, work really hard, and clearly benefit from working with me; I also learn a lot in such relationships and derive real satisfaction from seeing the difference I can make in the quality of their thinking and their work.

But, in this case, the relationship failed. Not because of its adventurous style but in the way so many teaching relations fall apart: more than once I told the student her work was not satisfactory; she did not accept my judgments and became increasingly suspicious and angry. And because so much passion had been invested in our relationship, the failure was particularly dramatic. The student felt let down, became outraged, and charged me with sexual harassment.

And because she did, the university had occasion to investigate my teaching practices. Although no evidence was found of the harassment the student claimed, the university looked at the pedagogical relation we had and decided it was against university rules.

As upsetting as it was to have someone I had worked so hard to help turn against me and accuse me of a loathsome crime, I am much more disturbed by the implications of the university's determination. Seeing a relation between a student enamored of a teacher's work, a student who wanted to be like that teacher, and the teacher who responded deeply to the student's desire to work with her, who wanted profoundly to help her do what she desired, the university deemed such a connection, passionate and involving so many personal hopes and dreams, an amorous relation.

And indeed it was.

In my formal response to the student's complaint, I used the psychoanalytic notion of "transference" to explain her relation to me. In psychoanalytic theory, transference is the human tendency to put people in the position our parents once held for us. It is a nearly universal response to people whose opinions of us have great authority, in particular doctors *and teachers.* Since our feelings about our parents include an especially powerful form of love, transference is undoubtedly an "amorous relation." But transference is also an inevitable part of any relationship we have to a teacher who really makes a difference.

In the official report on my case, the university recommends that in the future I should stop working with any student who has such a transference onto me. Which means that I would not work with any student who really believed I had something important to teach her. I would be forced to turn away precisely those students most eager to work with me, including those graduate students who come to the university where I teach expressly in order to work with me.

While I had vociferously opposed the consensual-relations policies before I was accused, I never dreamed how dangerous these policies could be. My case suggests the way the category of "amorous relations" can snowball. By moving from the restricted field of romantic love to the exceedingly wide field of relationships that are either social, personal, or involve intense feelings, what was originally a policy about sexual relations could become a policy restricting and chilling pedagogical relations.

At its most intense—and, I would argue, its most productive—the pedagogical relation between teacher and student is, in fact, a "consensual amorous relation." And if schools decide to prohibit not only sex but "amorous relations" between teacher and student, the "consensual amorous relation" that will be banned from our campuses might just be teaching itself.

3. Object of Intellectual Inquiry

A year before I was accused of sexual harassment, I began to organize a research conference on teacher-student sex. Both sex and pedagogy are central focuses of my scholarship, and this topic meant thinking about them together. The idea for the conference was triggered, of course, by the new consensual-relations policies. The policies represented a radical shift in our understandings of both sex and teaching; I thought it our job as intellectuals to study and discuss this paradigm shift we were living through. I wanted to sit down and think about this change with a range of scholars who had knowledge relevant to the question.

I planned to invite speakers from different fields with truly diverse viewpoints. I imagined brilliant feminist theorists explaining how student-teacher affairs were a covert form of harassment. Philosophers would take us back to Plato where we could study Socrates's erotic relations with his students. Psychologists could analyze the dynamics of student-teacher relations; anthropologists might give us a cross-cultural perspective on the subject. Historians could offer accounts of important pedagogical liaisons from other times. Literary critics would analyze teacher-student romances in literature, and film scholars would look at the portrayal of such relations in the movies.

I presented my idea to the advisory board of a research center at the university, a committee made up of

accomplished faculty from diverse fields. The proposal was received enthusiastically: several people suggested panel topics and speakers, no one spoke against the idea, and the conference was unanimously endorsed. The conference was to take place in a year and a half, and the center would provide the requisite financial and administrative support. Although I was pleased my proposal had been accepted, I was, to be honest, also daunted by the size of the task I had just offered to undertake.

A week or so later, the center director told me she heard that several feminist faculty members were upset about the conference. She and I both assumed this must be a misunderstanding: they must have imagined we were planning a celebration of teacher-student sex instead of a thoughtful consideration including all sides of the issue. We figured we need only meet with these faculty, explain what we really planned to do, and they surely would agree this was a good idea.

We did meet with them. But they hadn't misunderstood. They were opposed to any open discussion of teacher-student sex. They believed discussion of the issue would aid and abet sexual harassers. And that it would add to the suffering of students who had been victims of harassment.

Around the table, we were all women and all feminists. We knew each other as colleagues, had worked together and learned from each other. But now we were speaking two different languages. As I outlined the various intellectual reasons for the conference, they spoke angrily and sometimes tearfully about suffering students.

I was dumbfounded to hear my colleagues speak against the pursuit of knowledge. As if, in a university, there were more important things than learning. They seemed to feel it was their duty to suppress the pursuit of knowledge *for the sake of the students.*

We obviously held widely differing views of our duties as feminist educators. Those who opposed the conference thought it their duty to protect students, protect them from anything that would make them unhappy or remind them of painful experiences. We who were planning the conference considered it our primary duty to foster knowledge. Inasmuch as we were teachers, it was our responsibility to expose students to as much learning as possible. Protecting students from knowledge that would make them uncomfortable seemed ultimately a failure to teach them, placing some other relationship above our duty as their teachers.

All around that table were feminists; the students we were concerned about were women. Their stance implied that the women we teach are delicate and in need of protection. We on the other hand assumed that what women most need is knowledge and that women students are tough enough to learn.

The meeting was a disaster. No common ground was ever reached. Seeing our colleagues' response to the idea, those of us planning the conference realized that it could not be what we had envisioned, that we would not be able to produce an open atmosphere of discussion and exploration. Disappointed, we decided to scrap the conference on teacher-student sex. Instead, we would have a conference on what we thought would be a safer, more innocuous topic: pedagogy and the personal.

This new topic was recognizably feminist. Feminists who write about teaching have stressed the importance of the personal, both as content and as technique. Feminist teaching often involves connecting personal material and feelings to the subject matter, encouraging students to include personal content in discussion and writing assignments. Many feminist theorists of education even go so far as to make the ultimate standard of learning personal: learning should be judged by its effect on the person. Since feminist scholars are doing most of the research on the personal dimension of pedagogy, this would inevitably be a feminist conference.

The center director and I called another meeting, inviting feminist faculty from various departments, including those who had attended our first unsuccessful meeting. We hoped to gain broad support among campus feminists for the conference. We wanted to dispel the dissension produced by the original conference idea, and we also wanted to pick our colleagues' brains for ideas about whom we might invite to speak.

The meeting began productively. I outlined the idea for the conference, and people began suggesting topics and speakers. A woman from the philosophy department reported that a respected feminist philosopher was currently doing work on this subject (we got this philosopher to speak at the conference). An English professor thought we should have someone talking about the effects of the teacher's race on the classroom (she didn't have a speaker in mind, but she later agreed to present a paper on classroom dynamics when the teacher is black and the students white). Our colleagues were entering into the spirit of the conference and offering ideas we were able to use. This was just the sort of brainstorming session we had hoped for.

Then a sociologist raised her hand. I wanted a sociological perspective at the conference and was not myself very familiar with the field; so I hoped she had some names to offer. But this sociologist had not come to help us think of speakers.

She asked if we could guarantee that no student would suffer because of the conference. I figured that this woman, who had not been at the first meeting, was speaking out of her concern about the original topic and had somehow not realized that we were talking about a different conference. So I explained that it was precisely because of concerns such as hers that we had decided to give up our earlier controversial plan and replace it with this new topic. But my explanation seemed to make no difference; she continued to speak as if we were still planning a conference likely to upset students. The conference topic just didn't seem to register; nor did this feminist scholar seem to recognize that we were planning a decidedly feminist conference.

In fact, the sociologist was not, in this instance, speaking as a feminist scholar. She had just been appointed to head the university affirmative-action office, and she was speaking in her new official capacity. Because she had been a harsh critic of the administration's lax attitude toward sexual harassment, the chancellor had appointed her in order to show that the school was taking a new hard line on the problem. Her performance at this meeting was one of her very first acts in the campaign to get tough on harassment.

She spoke with the authority of her position, admonishing those of us planning the conference as if she had the right to discipline us. It was infuriating to hear someone still accusing me of endangering students after I had already given up the conference topic I really wanted in response to similar objections, objections that I considered wrongheaded. I was, moreover, offended by her tone and her presumption to reprimand. Finally, I lost my cool and roared "Fuck you!"; not long after, she left the meeting.

That evening I wrote her a note apologizing for losing my temper, explaining that I particularly regretted our fight because I had imagined that, as feminists, we were "on the same side." A bit later, on the occasion of my being named a distinguished professor, I received a note from the affirmative-action officer officially congratulating me on my honor (a matter for her office because, until my appointment, all the distinguished professors were men). She took the occasion to apologize for her conduct at the meeting. The two of us then met to smooth things over; she claimed she had been reacting to the first conference idea and made it clear that she had no objection to the new topic. I was, at the time, relieved by our rapprochement and willing to chalk the whole thing up to some bizarre mistake.

Now that I'm no longer concerned with the short-term goal of trying to assure my conference, I find myself once again, and more than ever, outraged by what the affirmative-action officer did at that meeting. Not by her confusion of the two different conference topics, but by the very fact that she considered it her duty to try and prevent any scholarly conference, whatever the topic.

Such a gesture represents a considerable departure from the usual domain of the overseer of campus equal opportunity. It suggests that she understood her charge to clean up the university as a mandate to expand substantially the purview of the office. If the affirmative-

action office can interrogate scholarly conferences, then its jurisdiction might include not only policing the treatment of people but actually shackling the pursuit of knowledge.

After the affirmative-action officer left the meeting, no one took up the opposition to the conference. On the contrary: the historian whom she had brought with her immediately began to offer suggestions as to how to find historians working on the topic. She tried hard to bring us back to the earlier, productive atmosphere, but the outburst of open hostility had been just too disruptive. We couldn't get going again and disbanded soon afterward.

Despite the meeting's dramatic breakdown, it did not seem that there was any substantial resistance to the new topic. So we proceeded to plan a conference called "Pedagogy: The Question of the Personal."

Participants came from across North America and

from a number of different disciplines: literature, sociology, philosophy, film, composition, and, of course, education. Some of the speakers were senior scholars of national reputation; one was a dean; others were promising young faculty; and several were graduate students, important to include so as to represent student perspectives on the topic. The presentations were lively and diverse: there was a screening of *The Prime of Miss Jean Brodie,* a talk on teaching as a Jew, and an ethnographic account of personal dynamics among high-energy physicists. It was a great conference, if I do say so myself.

While in many ways diverse, the conference was consistently feminist. Two sessions were specifically devoted to the effect of gender on teaching. And beyond those two sessions, nearly all the speakers in every session were, in fact, feminist scholars.

But there were also feminists out in the hall protesting the conference.

The protesters called themselves "Students Against Sexual Harassment" (SASH). This ad hoc organization had come into existence two months earlier at a meeting of graduate students from my department. The meeting had been convened by the students who had accused me of sexual harassment; they and their friends were calling for a boycott of the conference I was organizing.

As the conference began, SASH set up a table outside the room where we were meeting. They sold baked goods to conference participants; also for sale were bumper stickers sporting witticisms like "Distinguished Professors Do It Pedagogically." They positioned themselves at the door to the room and thrust a "fact sheet" about sexual harassment on our campus upon everyone who entered. The sheet told of the case against me even though it was still undergoing what was supposed to be a confidential investigation. Thus, feminists who had come to the conference from around the country learned that their convener had been accused of sexual harassment.

At the end of the first day, when the conference had reached full attendance, a student began distributing another handout to all who passed through the doors. That handout was entitled "A Call to Action" and ended by exhorting the reader: "You have in your power today, the ability to take a stand on sexual harassment in a concrete and meaningful way. Do not allow yourselves to be co-opted into Jane's deluded world. Make a statement: Boycott!"

After the conference, Students Against Sexual Harassment was never heard from again. There is, to be sure, plenty for students who are against sexual harassment to do on our campus: harassment is a real and prevalent problem there, as it is throughout a society where women tend to be viewed as sex objects. But

Students Against Sexual Harassment only ever did one thing. The only thing this organization ever did to combat sexual harassment was to protest a feminist scholarly conference.

All of the confrontations around my conference pitted feminist against feminist. While specifics and players varied—the conference topic changed; the protesters might be faculty, or administrators, or students—the positions were absolutely consistent. These positions play out a debate intrinsic to feminism, a crucial dialectic that repeats itself across feminism's history.

On the one hand, feminism is about the oppression of women. Women are not treated fairly in the world, and feminism attempts to remedy that: feminism thus necessarily speaks of women's misfortune. If women were not disadvantaged and disempowered, there would be no need for feminism.

On the other hand, feminism is about women's potential. If feminism could envision only women's lack of power, it would be a recipe for hopelessness rather than a dream that energizes us to change our lives and make the world better for women. Thus, feminism must speak of women's possibilities. If women were always and everywhere completely downtrodden, there would never have been any feminism.

This is the double foundation of feminism. While not

in theory contradictory, these two perspectives do tend to be experienced as contradictory. It seems difficult to think of women as both disadvantaged and forceful at one and the same time. Feminists are likely to take up one of these positions and cling to it to the exclusion of the other.

And so feminism continually finds itself splitting into opposing camps. One of these sides focuses on women's oppression; the other prefers to talk of women's liberation. Across the history of feminism, specifics and players vary, but the positions are consistent.

Some seventy years ago, after women got the vote, the women's movement divided over strategies to better women's condition: protectionism versus equal rights. Some veterans of the suffrage movement backed laws to protect women from working conditions that endangered women's health (supporting, for instance, weight limits on what women had to lift on the job). Other feminists opposed such laws, fearing they would keep women out of jobs that paid well and reinforce the notion that women were too fragile for certain occupations. These feminists lobbied for an equal-rights amendment. Rather than focusing on women's harsh conditions, the equal-rights supporters wanted to make sure that women were free to do whatever they could. But many feminists opposed the equal-rights amendment because they feared it would do nothing to remedy the special suffering and exploitation of women.

Today we can see these very same issues in operation. They reappear, for example, in the debates over whether there should be laws protecting women from the sterilizing effects of certain high-tech machines. On the one hand, we find a realistic concern for women's health; on the other, a fear that a paternalistic concern with women's bodies, especially our reproductive capacities, will deprive women of good jobs. Back in the 1920s the struggle between these positions was so divisive that it not only set veteran feminists against each other but played a major role in suspending the organized women's movement for half a century.

These days the feminist dialectic also appears in the guise of a pitched media battle: "power feminism" versus "victim feminism." Some vocal young feminists are complaining that the feminist focus on phenomena like date rape and sexual harassment is reinforcing the notion that women are victims. Rejecting a feminism that they see as stuck in an image of women's fragility, a feminism that's been dubbed "victim feminism," they propose that what women need is to recognize, enjoy, and enhance our power.

I must admit to sharing this preference for something like "power feminism," for a feminism that explores women's potential rather than emphasizes our restriction. But it troubles me to see that this new nineties "power feminism" frequently talks as if the worst enemies of women were other feminists, the wrong sort of feminists.

In the struggle to put a conference together, I got mad at feminist colleagues with different agendas than mine. In fact, I experienced these feminists, attuned to women's vulnerability and suffering, as my enemies. Feminist history makes me wary of this enmity and its angry, self-righteous pleasures. Feminist theory teaches me the necessity of both sorts of feminism, of the dialectic between them. History and theory together suggest that we think about whose interests it serves when feminists are at each other's throats.

Feminists are especially likely to turn against each other when the topic is sex. Here again we find the fundamental feminist dialectic—concern with oppression versus concern with liberation. And when sexual questions divide feminists, the arguments seem to get particularly heated.

Feminists widely agree that women's sexuality has been variously exploited, assaulted, deformed, condemned, and denied. But feminists have differed in their responses to the pervasiveness of a sexuality in which men are desiring subjects and women dehumanized objects. While some feminists view sexuality as a means of dehumanizing women, others of us believe we must claim our sexuality in order to be fully human. While some of us explore alternatives to the dominant form of sexuality, others seek ways of restricting male sexuality.

In the early 1980s a group of feminists organized an extremely effective campaign against pornography. They sponsored municipal ordinances in Minneapolis, Indianapolis, and a half dozen other cities. By 1985 their influence was such that the Attorney General's Commission on Pornography (better known as the Meese Commission) called on antiporn feminists to testify to the harm pornography does.

The campaign against pornography provided a strikingly visible and forceful instance of feminism at a moment when feminism's effect was otherwise becoming increasingly faint in a newly conservative political scene. This high-profile campaign led the lay public to assume that the antiporn position was held by all feminists. But, in fact, the campaign against pornography did not represent a feminist consensus.

While feminists generally agree that pornography is usually sexist, most feminists do not see it as essentially more sexist than other parts of the culture, such as great literature, advertising, or the bridal industry. Singling out pornography as *the* target for feminism makes it likely that the wrong will be understood not as sexism but as sexuality per se. Many feminists worried that singling out such an explicitly sexual form of sexism would play into the hands of the reactionary and antifeminist movement for traditional morality.

As it turned out, there was indeed reason to worry. In Indianapolis, the feminist antiporn ordinance was sponsored by a conservative legislator on record against gay rights and the Equal Rights Amendment. In Suffolk County, New York, the ordinance was introduced by a council member whose stated goal was to protect women, to "restore them to what ladies used to be." And the Meese Commission ultimately used feminist testimony to support its own conservative agenda.

In 1982, as the feminist antiporn movement was reaching full force, Barnard College announced a feminist conference on sexuality. The conference was attacked in advance by Women Against Pornography (WAP), the largest and most successful antiporn group, the feminist organization that, three years later, would testify for the Meese Commission.

The conference was the ninth in a yearly series Barnard called "The Scholar and the Feminist." The series title expresses the double commitment of the conferences, to scholarship and to feminism. The 1982 sexuality conference was no different: it was a serious, scholarly event and, although topics and perspectives were diverse, all the presentations were unmistakably feminist.

Women Against Pornography did what they could to get the conference canceled and, on the day of the conference, showed up to picket and leaflet. The protest treated the participants neither as scholars nor as feminists. The conference nevertheless distinguished itself both by the wealth of research gathered there and by the range of feminist perspectives on the subject, a range that included WAP's view of sexuality as a primary site of women's oppression. But the protest ignored both the value of the research and the wide range of viewpoints, targeting instead a few speakers, claiming they were perverts and enemies of women. True to the organization's name, the women protested as if the conference were pornography.

The Barnard conference occurred at a moment when the antiporn movement threatened to monopolize the feminist conversation about sex. According to Carole Vance, who organized the conference, the objective was to "keep the sexuality conversation open." To my mind, this commitment to an open conversation bespeaks these feminists' commitment to scholarship. An open conversation, which considers an issue in a way not predetermined by received notions of right and wrong, is absolutely essential to intellectual exploration. "Keeping the conversation open" may in fact be synonymous with intellectual inquiry.

The Barnard conference's commitment was to the

possibility of being *both* a scholar *and* a feminist. WAP's attack, however, makes "the scholar and the feminist" into an opposition: the scholar versus the feminist. Impugning a scholarly conference in the name of feminism, WAP made it seem like one had to choose between feminism and scholarship, between toeing a feminist line and pursuing intellectual inquiry.

A decade after the Barnard sexuality conference, I tried to organize a conference with the same objective: to keep a sex conversation open. I felt that the anti-harassment movement had monopolized the conversation on teacher-student sex, and I wanted there to be an open discussion of the topic rather than just moral certainty and silence.

In the 1980s feminists targeted pornography and created a revival of feminism as a movement with wide social influence. In the 1990s, sexual harassment has replaced pornography as the high-profile feminist issue. Like pornography, harassment allows feminists to reach a broad audience. Like pornography, the focus on harassment runs the risk of being widely misunderstood as an objection to sexuality rather than sexism. And like pornography, the issue of harassment seems to produce a protectionist feminism that objects to intellectual inquiry.

The 1982 Barnard conference protest is a landmark in the history of feminism. An influential feminist organization took it upon itself to protest a major feminist conference. While the conference I organized a decade later and its little protest were neither of the scale nor of the significance of this historic feminist confrontation, I am nonetheless struck by the parallels. Just as Women Against Pornography treated the feminist sexuality conference as if it were pornography, Students Against Sexual Harassment implied that our conference on pedagogy was a form of sexual harassment.

In November 1992—five months before the pedagogy conference took place and nine months after the planning session where the affirmative-action officer walked out—two students went to the office of affirmative action and filled out forms to charge me with sexual harassment. The official "Complaint of Discrimination" form they used includes a section entitled "Resolution Sought" where the complainant lists what she would have the university do to remedy her situation. Both my accusers filled out the Resolution Sought section with a list of four nearly identical items. Both asked that I be reprimanded, that I be kept out of any decisions regarding their work, and that the department create a mechanism to deal with sexual harassment. These three demands are pretty standard on such complaints, but both my complainants also included an extraordinary fourth demand.

I mention this demand last because it is so unusual, but, in fact, both complainants actually put what I'm calling a "fourth demand" *first* on their lists, as if *this* were more important to them than protecting themselves or punishing me. Under the heading Resolution Sought, one student wrote: "1. That the respondent understand that making the complaint the subject of intellectual inquiry constitutes retaliation." The other student went even a little further: "1. That the respondent understand that making this claim *any aspect* of intellectual inquiry constitutes retaliation."

Let me gloss this legalese: "the respondent" here means me. The complainants want me to understand that, should I make their complaints the subject of my research—should I, *in any way,* touch upon them in my research—that would in and of itself be considered "retaliation." Part of the university's affirmative-action policy is a promise to protect complainants against retaliation, to protect even those whose complaints are found to be baseless. So when these complaints define research as retaliation, they put the university under an obligation to prohibit research.

The affirmative-action office helped the complainants fill out these forms. And the office accepted this attempt to constrain my research as a legitimate possible "resolution" to the case. In effect, these requests extend the jurisdiction of the affirmative-action office to include intellectual inquiry.

When first I read the complaints, I understood these demands as an attempt to ensure that I wouldn't write about the case. Since my research was precisely concerned with the interrelation of teaching, feminism, and sex, it seemed quite likely that I would want to use this experience in my writing. And so I worried that the university could stifle my scholarly writing.

Because I assumed the students were mainly concerned to protect their identities, in an early attempt to mediate, I offered to promise that if ever I wrote about the case, I would guarantee the complainants' anonymity. This was, of course, before they began calling meetings, contacting the press, handing out fact sheets, and otherwise publicly proclaiming that they had filed harassment charges against me. Once they went public, I realized that their attempt to constrain my work had nothing to do with protecting their identities.

But it was not until the investigation was concluded that I realized how dangerous these demands were. They were not just asking the university to restrict my writing, not just asking that it inhibit my speech. The university was ultimately being asked to police my thinking.

In no way was I to take the case as an object of intellectual inquiry. That is to say, I was not to study it nor derive knowledge from it; I was, in other words, not to think about the case.

As it turns out, the university decided not to forbid

my taking the case as an object of intellectual inquiry. But then I was not found guilty of sexual harassment. Had I been, it is conceivable that the university might have taken it upon itself to ban the very book you are reading.

4. Professor Accused of Kissing Students

The conference I organized proved impossible to disentangle from the sexual harassment case brought against me. Despite concerted effort to keep them separate, the conference became an intrinsic part of the story. Conference and case appeared together in media accounts, and I certainly couldn't tell of the case without bringing in the conference.

At the time of the event, this exasperated me: I did not see why the conference had to be contaminated by the accusations. Now maybe I do see why. Perhaps it was, in a certain way, appropriate for my accusers to target the conference. Not, of course, for the reasons they gave, not because the conference was any sort of justification for either sexual harassment or my behavior. But because *another conference,* in fact, lay at the very heart of the accusations against me.

Both of the complaints actually pinpoint the harassment as beginning on the same day—Friday, April 19, 1991. Even though my relation to both students had been personalized and sexualized long before April, their complaints alleged that it was on April 19 that they began to consider my behavior sexual harassment. All three of us spent that entire day attending a research conference held at our university.

My alleged sexual harassment arose at one academic conference and eventually got entangled with another conference. From beginning to end, the case against me was bound up with conferences. I take that finally as no coincidence. Rather, I would argue that the behavior that got me accused of sexual harassment has everything to do with academic conferences in general.

Academics go to conferences to share research, to find out what others working on the same problems have come up with, to teach and to learn. But a conference is not just an intellectual or professional event; such gatherings are profoundly social. At conferences, scholars who usually make contact by reading each other's publications get together in person: we share meals and have drinks together, stay up late talking, or meet early for breakfast.

At their best, conferences realize my vision of intellectual community. The excitement of sharing our life's work cannot be separated from the pleasure of contact with people who are devoted to the same thing. In such a context, the intellectual is entwined with the social, the professional inextricable from the personal.

Conferences are also inevitably sexual. It is not uncommon for scholars to have affairs during conferences, even more common to engage in flirtations. When the possibility of intellectual communion arises in contacts with real flesh-and-blood people, the excitement and the connection can turn explicitly sexual. A good conference is likely to be an eroticized workplace.

As both my accusers tell it, it was at a conference that my behavior became sexual harassment. The conference in question was a gay and lesbian studies conference held in April 1991 at the university where I teach.

This was a good conference. Many of the papers were smart and most were daring, pushing the academic envelope. Discussion was lively and engaged. Gay and lesbian studies was a new field, and the gathering was high on the prospect of bold possibility.

Like most conferences, the schedule included explicitly social events as well as work sessions. Saturday night, the conference closed with a party at a beautiful old mansion owned by the university where we could continue to talk, warmed by food and drink. Although this last event was very much part of the conference, its culmination in fact, it also felt very much like what it was—a Saturday night party.

At the end of the evening, a graduate student from another university, who had presented an aggressive theoretical polemic the preceding day, came up to me, told me she had seen me lecture at her school two years earlier, complimented me on my legs, and asked if I wanted to go back to her hotel room with her. I was flattered but graciously declined.

Although the invitation surprised me, it didn't seem like some untoward anomaly. It felt rather in keeping with the general atmosphere at this conference—a conference that was sexier than most. The field was young and vital; the topic was sexuality. You couldn't separate the intellectual energy from the sexual. Not only were participants flirting in the corridors between sessions, during the sessions they were flirting in the very act of posing questions and making associations.

This was my first gay studies conference. Yet it felt deeply familiar. As a student, I had been active in gay liberation. Gay liberation on our campus had been intertwined with feminism; the women who participated were all active student feminists. But there was one important difference between feminism and the gay movement in the early seventies: while women's liberation was building women's studies, there wasn't anything like gay studies. Now, twenty years later, I was witnessing the growth of gay and lesbian studies, and I relished its connection to my student activism.

The conference took me back to 1971. Not only because that was the year I joined the campus gay organization, the year I made love to a woman for the first time. The real connection to 1971 was less abstract and more palpable: the energy and sense of a bright future felt ever so much like women's studies twenty years earlier. Once again I was surrounded by bold young women, exploring the possibilities of a new mix of political, intellectual, and sexual liberation. Here was liberation at its most rewarding: women being smart and gutsy together. I felt like I had come home to that sense of community that had guided me for years as a feminist scholar. I was grateful to feel the heat of feminism around me again and to feel anew my own energy and desire for the possibilities liberation might bring.

This was not just any old gay and lesbian conference; this was the First Annual Graduate Student Gay and Lesbian Conference. This was not only my first gay conference; it was my first time at a graduate student conference. The latter category seemed to me exotic and unfamiliar. When I was a student, there was no such thing. But in the nineties, graduate students with an increasing sense of professional identity were organizing conferences at which all the presenters, usually with the exception of big-name keynote speakers, were students. Faculty attendance was desired (I had been asked to moderate two panels), but the purpose was to showcase student work.

Gay and lesbian studies was a young field and, as is often the case with a new field, some of the best work was being done by graduate students. The papers at this conference were much better than the academic norm—smarter, more original, and more daring. Here was intellectual inquiry as it ought to be. Since I'd never been to either a grad student or a gay conference, I didn't know which category to credit.

Actually, I figured it was precisely the combination of the two that made the conference the event it was. I wanted to express my admiration for this fortuitous conjunction, my sense of how grad students and queer studies were, in fact, a perfect match. Everyone seemed so clever and sassy; I wanted to rise to the occasion. So, in the heat of the moment, in the process of phrasing a question for one of the speakers (a really good-looking woman from out of town), I came out with the statement: "graduate students are my sexual preference."

The statement was meant to be a joke. We were at the first ever Graduate Student Gay and Lesbian Conference, a conference distinguished by a unique conjunction of identities—one institutional, the other sexual. The joke was playing with these two identities, trying loosely to suggest that "graduate student" was somehow like "gay and lesbian." The two categories worked so well together at this conference that it seemed fun to imagine more intimate connections.

Of course, as with any joke, deeper truths lay behind the wordplay. The truth behind this joke was my very real passion for graduate students. Of all my professional interactions, working with graduate students is what matters most to me, what provides me with the most satisfaction, and what continues to give me the impetus to teach and research as well as I can. I get more intellectually from interactions with graduate students than I do from undergraduates or from colleagues. So graduate students are my "preference."

I termed that preference "sexual" to make a facetious connection with gay and lesbian. But in calling it "sexual" I also meant something more serious. At heart a Freudian, I believe that our professional impulses are sublimated sexual drives. The pleasure I get from working with graduate students, the intensity of my wish that certain promising graduate students will choose to work with me, and the satisfaction I get from seeing the imprint of my teaching in their work all strongly suggest a sexual analogy.

I was trying too hard to be clever; no one got the joke. It was certainly not the first time I had embarrassed myself in a professional forum by telling a joke that flopped. But my bad jokes had never had such serious repercussions.

Both accusations of sexual harassment take my sexual preference statement as a point of departure. The students claimed that the statement completely altered their perception of my behavior: it made them think I was trying to sleep with them. Both my complainants and many of their fellow students took my statement as a public announcement that I fucked graduate students. And, based on this newly revealed "truth" about me, they reinterpreted all my behavior that previously had not troubled them.

My statement was taken as an instance of sexual harassment because it was thought to indicate that I treated graduate students as objects, that I didn't respect them, that I didn't care about their minds and was only interested in their bodies. The irony is that, whereas students heard my statement as demeaning, I had seldom felt so much respect for students. And I naively thought that in *this* context a "sexual preference" statement could be heard as an expression of admiration and esteem.

On April 19, 1991, I didn't know how I had been misunderstood. I made the remark in the late morning and spent the rest of the day at the conference surrounded by graduate students. No one said anything to me about my statement; no one seemed offended. I remained completely and pleasurably immersed in the conference. There were plenty more good papers to hear, and I continued to pose questions during formal discussions as well as have lively conversations between sessions, doing my best to participate in the energetic intellectual exchange around me.

The last session of the day ended at 9 P.M. As I was leaving, a group of graduate students invited me to go with them to a local lesbian bar. I went along, wanting to prolong the feel of the day.

One of the students in the group was my advisee. The previous semester she had written a creative, experimental paper for a seminar she was taking with me. In that paper she interwove love letters to an unnamed woman with an analysis of my most recent scholarly book, which contains a discussion of love letters between women. The paper was daring not only because it was graphically sexual but because she was taking on her teacher's writing. And now she was going to present this same paper at the conference; it was slated for the next morning.

At the bar, she and I found ourselves—as we had so many times before—in a heated conversation about the erotic dynamics of our pedagogical relation. I did research on the erotics of pedagogy, and it was also a topic she wanted to pursue, hence the paper she was presenting. But these conversations were also very personal. We were not discussing sex, power, and pedagogy in the abstract; we were inevitably thinking of our own highly charged relationship.

This conversation was like so many we had had, but it was also different. The context of the conference, the excitement of a long day of intellectual and personal stimulation were pushing our standard conversation to a new level of intensity. And it was heightened further still by our acute awareness that, in a few hours, she was going to be taking the topic of our pedagogical relation explicitly into the conference.

A group of women got up to dance together; my student invited me to join them. We all danced in a circle, reminding me of the women's group dancing of the early seventies. Although I had decided years ago that I was not a very good dancer and should stick to talking, in this context I was happy to participate in yet another reminder of the feminist pleasures of my student days.

When the dance was over, my advisee told me she

was leaving. I had come to the bar with her and her friends, but I didn't want to leave yet. I found someone else who could give me a ride home and told my student I was staying. I wanted to prolong the conference day as much as possible, and I was going to stay at the bar as long as anyone from the conference was there.

She was leaving and I was staying; so we said good-bye. It had been our custom for some while to embrace upon parting. She had initiated this a few months earlier: she was dropping me off at my house and got out of her truck and asked if we could hug. Now we hugged and kissed whenever we said good-bye. But this time was different.

Our embrace would be witnessed by the assembled conference participants; it would be remembered the next day when she gave her paper about the erotics of our pedagogical relationship. The sense of an audience totally transformed our conventional gesture. In such a context, our customary, familiar embrace could not help but become a loaded performance.

We both were known to enjoy making spectacles of ourselves, and this opportunity for professional exhibitionism was bound to turn us on. We didn't say anything to each other, but somehow the usual good-bye peck suddenly became a real kiss.

I don't actually know who started it. I know it surprised me and seemed to occur simultaneously to both of us, as if spontaneously generated out of the moment. In any case, whichever of us actually initiated this torrid kiss, both of us were clearly into it.

It was a performance. By that, I do not mean that I wasn't really kissing her or that I didn't find it sexy. What I mean is that we didn't just happen to be seen kissing, but we kissed like that because we knew we were being watched. And it was precisely the knowledge of being watched that made it sexy.

I thought of the kiss as very much part of the conference, a sort of advance commentary on her paper the next day. I fancied that the kiss embodied a question about lesbian studies, trying to imagine "lesbian studies" not just as studies about lesbians or even studies by lesbians, but as a way of studying that is in itself somehow "lesbian," imbued with desire between women. To my mind, our student-teacher kiss enacted a fantasy of lesbian pedagogy: women together tasting from the forbidden tree of knowledge.

The kiss was brazen and public—and thus particularly appropriate for a conference distinguished by its intellectual and sexual daring. This was a performance tailor-made for the First Annual Graduate Student Gay and Lesbian Conference, whose title, after all, was "Flaunting It."

I thought I was back in 1971. Not that I thought I was a student again. But I thought I was back in a space where feminist professors and students, joined by a common pursuit of liberation, could play with our institutional roles rather than be limited by them.

I was wrong. I might have imagined it was 1971, but it was very much 1991. And the sight of a professor and a student kissing didn't signify sexy, new feminist pedagogical possibilities; it signified sexual harassment. It didn't matter that I was a woman; it didn't matter that I was a feminist; it didn't matter that we were at a conference exploring sexuality; it didn't matter that the student was obviously into this public display. All those connotations were obliterated by the fact that I was a professor and she a student.

I was, admittedly, trying to be outrageous. But I believed that I was in the company of other outrageous women, women who shared my ambition to flout conventional notions of propriety. I certainly did not think I was offending my student; I thought of her as a sort of partner in crime, likewise interested in being publicly appreciated as outrageous. Nothing she said or did that evening or for many months afterward suggested to me that she had any other relation to our joint performance.

But, a year and a half later, she charged me with sexual harassment. By then she no longer was my student, and we hadn't spoken in months. Her complaint alleged that she was upset by the kiss but had been too intimidated to tell me.

If she were upset, she showed no sign of it at the time. Whatever her real feelings might have been, those who witnessed the kiss saw her as a willing and even eager participant. And she was well aware of how it had looked. So aware that, when she decided to accuse me of harassment, she worried that the kiss would contradict her claim that I had subjected her to *unwanted* sexual advances.

She needn't have worried. In the climate of the nineties, our engagement in a *consensual* sexual relation (albeit one that lasted no more than a minute and didn't go below the neck) could actually function as "proof" of harassment. By the time she lodged her complaint, the question of whether her participation was willing or not didn't much matter. Professor/student sex had become more or less synonymous with sexual harassment.

On April 19, 1993, two years to the day after I kissed my advisee in a bar, the official student newspaper at our school ran the front-page banner headline: "Professor Accused of Kissing Students."

The article reports that an investigation was being conducted by the university affirmative-action office "into allegations that a female professor kissed two female students." According to the paper's informant (an unnamed faculty member in my department), "two female students have filed complaints about Jane Gallop, alleging that she kissed them."

The facts here are a tad confused. While there were indeed two complaints against me, I had only kissed one student. And that student didn't go to the affirmative-action office to complain that I'd kissed her. She went to claim that I tried to sleep with her and that, when she turned me down, I started rejecting her work. She filed her complaint in tandem with another student who made almost identical claims against me, even though I never kissed *her*. Both women charged me with classic quid pro quo sexual harassment.

The article, however, never mentions sexual harassment. In the student newspaper version of things, the kiss looms so large that it is sufficient in and of itself to complain about. The article consults a paralegal from the university legal clinic who suggests that kissing "could be considered sexual contact" and that "if the students did not consent, the situations might be considered fourth-degree sexual assaults."

And if the students *had* consented? "Even if the two students did consent," the article goes on to say, "Gallop broke a university policy." The policy in question is quoted from the university's student handbook: "Consenting amorous or sexual relationships between instructor and student are *unacceptable*."

This student newspaper account is almost comically ill-informed. The facts are muddled, the issue of sexual harassment is left out, and it looks like the affirmative-action office monitors not discrimination or even harassment but kissing. Yet, as silly as the article seemed, it was onto something.

At a moment when the investigator, the complainants, their supporters, my lawyer, and I were all focused on whether or not I was guilty of sexual harassment, the student newspaper completely ignored the entire question of harassment. Instead it focused exclusively on the kiss, treated it as if it were a sex act, and thus was led to the very policy that would ultimately determine the case.

At the time this article appeared, none of the principals in the case considered this policy applicable. But the investigation was still confidential, and the student reporter talked to no one directly involved—neither to the complainants, nor to the accused, nor to the investigator. He was ignorant of all our various complex and involved understandings and, perhaps *because* of his ignorance, he managed correctly to predict the official finding—eight months later—of "consenting amorous relationship."

The complainants were accusing me of serious crimes—sexual harassment, discrimination, and abuse of power—not of something as petty and ambiguous as a kiss. And even though I had kissed one student and not the other, they nevertheless insisted that I had treated them both the same. But the university begged to differ.

The official determination dismissed one complaint as improbable, while finding me at fault in the other. From the point of view of the university, one somewhat lengthy kiss made all the difference.

In its final determination, the university proved the silly, misinformed student newspaper version right. Although I had been accused of sexual harassment, the crime I was found guilty of was kissing students.

Nearly a year after the student newspaper article appeared, a local, left-leaning, countercultural weekly ran a wrap-up of the university investigation. Although this account only treats one of the complaints against me—the one by the student I *had* kissed—its coverage is otherwise thorough. Appearing after the investigation had been completed, this article was not hampered by the strictures meant to preserve confidentiality. The reporter had read the official determination and had interviewed both me and my accuser at length.

The article was written by the paper's news editor, who not only had been following the case for a year but had for several years been writing pieces exposing sexual harassment at the university. By dint of his muckraking, he had become a local expert on academic sex discrimination, harassment, and the doings of the affirmative-action office. With all this background, he produced a serious and well-informed account of the case.

Explicitly stating that "the case revolved around much more than the kiss," this article allots the kiss just one sentence. But that single sentence—while noting that the principals downplay the kiss—contends that the act is central to the case. Right next to the article, the weekly ran an eye-catching sidebar (boxed-in and shaded gray), devoted exclusively to the kiss.

Because the kiss is central, the paper features it. Because it is not supposed to be central, it is relegated to a sidebar. Incidental to the case proper, the case the complainants tried to make, the kiss is central to what the case nonetheless became. The flashy sidebar aptly represents the contradictory status of this kiss: tangential *and* prominent, both incidental and central.

The sidebar is signed with initials that match the article's byline. The local muckraker used a double strategy to cover the case. Not only did he produce two separate items to run side by side, but the two pieces present a striking contrast in tone.

The article proper is temperate, careful and balanced—perhaps even a bit too dry owing to its concentration on administrative procedure. On the other hand, the sidebar opens sensationally by quoting from the description of the kiss found in the student's complaint: "She mashed her lips against mine and shoved her tongue in my mouth."

Benefiting from the student's stylistic proclivity to pulp fiction, the sidebar portrays me as a literal as well as a figurative "masher." (A masher is "a man who attempts to force his amorous attentions upon a woman," my dictionary tells me.) And the reader is treated to a classic pulp kiss: a passive and innocent victim, an aggressor, violent verbs, images of forced penetration.

This is blatant sensationalism. It squeezes all the sex and violence it can out of what was, after all, just a kiss.

The sidebar infuriated me. It was excruciating to read this lurid description of myself, to think everyone in town was reading it. I fantasized turning public humiliation into superiority by getting up on my high-cultural horse, despising sensationalism and railing against exploitation. I imagined retaliating by unleashing a stock academic rant about the media, its pandering and lack of seriousness.

But, in this case, an attack on sensationalism was not going to work.

After all, it wasn't the media who made the kiss into a spectacle. That's what it was in the first place.

Sensationalism actually may be the most appropriate way to report the kiss, the best way to transmit its effect as provocative spectacle. The problem with the sidebar is not the sensationalism per se, but the way the flamboyant spectacle is split off from the serious treatment of the case. The sidebar literally takes the kiss out of context, isolating it from the larger story.

The article proper fulfills the journalist's responsibility to inform; the sidebar produces pleasure and excitement. While the split coverage implies that one effect has nothing to do with the other, the double coverage suggests they could really be linked.

People have been railing against sensationalism for at least as long as there have been newspapers. The fact that the complaint is as old as journalism itself suggests that it may not be possible or desirable to inform the public without also arousing sensations.

A journalist's responsibility is not unlike a professor's: both of us do research and transmit knowledge. To accuse a journalist of sensationalism is pretty much the equivalent of accusing a professor of sexualizing her teaching.

Sensationalism is not in and of itself bad journalism; it becomes bad precisely when sensation is split off from knowledge, when pleasure is procured at the expense of imparting knowledge. The same could be said about teaching. Sexy teaching is not in and of itself harassment. Sexual harassment occurs when sex is split off from teaching, when pleasure is procured at the expense of imparting knowledge.

Like the crusade to desexualize teaching, the attack on sensationalism involves fundamental assumptions about the relation between sex and knowledge. Both campaigns treat the incompatibility of sex and knowledge as a foregone conclusion: if it's sexy, it must not be knowledge.

Both campaigns are thus doomed to failure. It is no more possible to really teach without at times eliciting powerful and troubling sensations than it is to write powerfully without producing the same sort of sensations.

Teachers and writers might better serve the claims of knowledge if we were to resist not sex but the impulse to split off sex from knowledge.

When I said that graduate students were my sexual preference, when I kissed my advisee in a bar for all to see, I was making a spectacle of myself. And, at the same time, I was being a teacher.

The performance turned me on and was meant to

turn my audience on, literally and figuratively. The spectacle was meant to shock and entertain, and to make people think.

I gave this book a tabloid title because I wanted, again, to make a spectacle of myself. When I told friends of the title, they worried that the book would be mistaken for sensationalism rather than a thoughtful consideration of important issues.

In fact, I'm hoping to produce a sensation. Not the hollow kind where sensation is achieved at the expense of thought. But the best kind, where knowledge and pleasure, sex and thought play off and enhance each other.

When I kissed my student at a conference, I was trying to produce just such a spectacle. But I failed to make myself understood.

By writing this book, I thought I'd give it another shot.

Jane Gallop is Professor of English and Comparative Literature at the University of Wisconsin at Milwaukee. She is the author of numerous books including *Around 1981: Academic Feminist Literary Theory* and *Thinking Through the Body*. She is also the editor of *Pedagogy: The Question of Impersonation*.

Library of Congress Cataloging-in-Publication Data

Gallop, Jane

Feminist accused of sexual harassment / Jane Gallop.

p. cm. — (Public planet books)

ISBN 0-8223-1925-X (cloth : alk. paper). — ISBN 0-8223-1918-7 (pbk. : alk. paper)

1. Sexual harassment in universities and colleges—United States. 2. Feminism and education—United States. 3. Gallop, Jane, 1952–. 4. Women college teachers—United States—Biography. 5. Feminists—United States—Biography. I. Title. II. Series.

LC212.862.G35 1997

370.19'345—dc20 96-35150 CIP